MW00975060

Finding Healing
in Times of
Grief and Loss

Caring Companions
from Abbey Press

Finding Healing
in Times of
Grief and Loss

Edited by Silas Henderson

Abbey Press Publications
St. Meinrad, IN 47577

Text © 2015 Saint Meinrad Archabbey
Published by Abbey Press Publications
St. Meinrad, Indiana 47577
www.abbeypresspublications.com

Cover and book design by Mary E. Bolin.

The Scripture quotations contained herein are from the
New Revised Standard Version Bible, copyright © 1989 by
the Division of Christian Education of the National Council
of the Churches of Christ in the U.S.A. Used by permission.

Library of Congress Control Number
2014959555

ISBN 978-0-87029-676-5

Printed in the United States of America.

Introduction

In her book, *Grief Therapy*, Karen Katafiasz encourages the reader, "Respect the power of grief. Know that it can affect you psychologically, physically, and spiritually in intense and sometimes surprising ways. Stay gentle with yourself." This is sage advice and an important reminder of the significant ways that grief can impact each one of us.

The five authors in this volume all speak to the ways that we can enter into the experience of grief and come through with hearts and spirits renewed by the cherished memories of the one we've lost. Whether the passing of our dear one was recent or further in the past, peace is always possible.

Bringing together five of our most celebrated *CareNotes*, it is our hope that *Finding Healing in Times of Grief and Loss* will provide help and hope to you and your families as you remember and celebrate the life and memory of those who have gone before.

—Silas Henderson

Contents

༄

CHAPTER I

Grieving With a Grateful Heart

By Lisa Irish

How does one take a deep breath when the clenching pain of loss wraps around your chest? How does one see the blue sky or hear the morning birds greet the rising sun when all one can see or hear is emptiness? A grieving heart gets lost in a land of denial and loneliness and cannot reconnect, or even imagine, the experiences of love that were sown long before. Those moments of intimacy, of connection, and of life together are no longer strands of love that created this specific relationship. They become sources of pain, reminders of what is missing.

Janet deeply missed Tom, her husband of 42 years. She could not, and on some days would not, imagine life without him. She chose to ask for help, though, and joined a bereavement support group at our hospital. She faithfully attended week after week, to share her feelings and to listen to new friends in the group. On the last night, after a gentle collage-making activity, she said, "I just figured something out. All this time I have been coming here and talking about Tom, I have been honoring him. How grateful I am he was part of my life."

Working your way through | Janet's sadness was not immediately transformed that night. She still hurt, deeply, from Tom's absence. Yet something shifted when she opened her heart to gratitude, when she began to consider the gift of this relationship as she moved forward in her life. When seeds of gratitude are planted, we become open to another point of view. The devastating experience of loss is still present; but with time, awareness, and nurturing, a grateful heart beats within the broken places and brings healing. The memory of our loved one becomes a source of life, not just a reminder of loss. Read on as we highlight attitudes and actions that might be helpful in cultivating grateful grieving.

∾ *Saying "Thank you."* Most of us were trained as little children to say these two words, and we often repeated them without thinking. As adults, though, we might bring more awareness to the "thank you" opportunities in our daily life. The beauty of creation or the kindness of others all provide opportunities for giving thanks.

Cultivating this habit can help us practice gratitude when facing our loss, as well. For example, a glance at the desk and empty chair reminded Janet that her husband was no longer there to manage their finances. In the midst of this painful memory, she was able to remind herself of his hard work for their family. She opened her broken heart and offered a silent "thank you" to Tom. This simple statement became an intention and slowly, became a prayer, as she realized the love that was and is still present. With awareness, "thank you" becomes a doorway into living in the present moment, bringing love alongside.

Gratitude unlocks the fullness of life. It turns what we have into enough, and more. It turns denial into acceptance, chaos into order, confusion into clarity. It can turn a meal into a feast, a house into a home, a stranger into a friend. Gratitude makes sense of our past, brings peace for today and creates a vision for tomorrow.

—Melody Beattie,
The Language of Letting Go Journal

∽ *Embrace the legacy.* Sometimes people will say, "She wouldn't want me to be sad," relying upon that sentiment as a motivation to "be strong" and "get better." This approach can be challenging, because sadness is a natural response to loss. It cannot be rationalized away. Drawing upon the memory of our loved ones, though, is a good place to develop another pathway to healing through grateful grieving.

> "*I* still miss those I loved who are no longer with me, but I find I'm grateful I loved them. The gratitude has finally conquered the loss."
>
> —Rita Mae Brown,
> *Starting from Scratch*

When Mark lost his mother Gloria, he experienced her absence at every turn. The hardest time for him was the holiday season when his mom was the center of the family as Christmas approached. After many stories and tears, Mark came to an idea that created a link between his mom's memory and the rest of his life. He pulled out her Christmas cookie recipes, all her bowls and utensils, and brought his children into the kitchen. Together they made "Grandma's cookies" while sharing memories of this woman they all loved and missed.

This yearly ritual planted a seed in Mark's family. They experienced the healing gifts found through actively remembering Gloria's place in their lives and looked for new ways to share her legacy with the family. Their hearts discovered new expressions of gratitude for Gloria. Her legacy brought healing comfort in their grieving.

❧ *Trust the rhythms of grief.* The seasons often provide a template for grief. After a loss, we find ourselves identifying with the "letting go" associated with autumn or with feeling frozen in the long darkness of winter. Spring also offers helpful imagery as a season of "fits and starts." One day the temperature is warm, the next day it is much cooler, the next day brings rain. People are often impatient with spring, wanting the bitter cold and resulting restrictions of winter to stop. But spring isn't like that; it has its own rhythm that is often unexpected.

Spring, like grief, brings the unexpected. At the same time, since spring follows winter, it ultimately offers relief from winter's harshness, and brings waves of warmth after the chill. A grieving heart that seeks gratitude learns to notice similar transitions. The empty ache is eased by remembering a loved one's generosity, for example, filling the space with love. Memories and love become the relief and warmth sought after the cold of loss. They become sources of comfort that smooth the painful path of grieving. Experience them as gifts. Pause, notice, and be grateful for those moments of respite as they contribute to the healing process.

❧ *Transforming the connections.* When grieving is focused on absence, we are engulfed in experiences of emptiness and yearning. Nothing will fill the space left by our loved one. While this emotional state makes sense immediately following the death, it can become a life-limiting pattern as the months and years go by. Grieving that includes gratitude, however, transforms the connection between us and the beloved. We establish a life-giving connection that helps us move into our lives with the blessing and encouragement of those we have lost.

Sadie had dear memories of growing up on a farm with her sister Jewell. They explored creatures and creation as far as their young legs

> *All that we can know about those we have loved and lost is that they would wish us to remember them with a more intensified realization of their reality. What is essential does not die but clarifies. The highest tribute to the dead is not grief but gratitude.*
>
> —Thornton Wilder,
> *Our Town*

would take them. Jewell's untimely death propelled Sadie into a "fix-it" mentality that kept her constantly busy at work, at church, and in her home with a husband and three children. If she kept busy, Sadie reasoned, she'd feel better. She carefully avoided working in her garden or taking the long walks the two sisters had enjoyed as children. Sadie's life-limiting choices interfered with the sweet, albeit painful, memories of her childhood and of Jewell. As she developed a practice of gratitude, however, Sadie began to remember and treasure the connection to nature she shared with her sister. When she dug in the dirt or walked around the neighborhood, she found herself feeling closer to Jewell, somehow connected. These became life-giving choices for Sadie that filled her heart, not just her time.

Take Heart | "Death ends a life, not a relationship," wrote Mitch Albom as he was trying to sort out the dying and death of his beloved mentor, Morrie. He discovered that the lessons and love found in that relationship would live on and be part of who he was and how he chose to live his life. In this process, Mitch cultivated a grateful heart and experienced the fruits of grateful grieving.

The losses we face are devastating. The relationships can never be replaced. And yet, that side of ourselves that was alive around him or her can find new life through the practice of grateful grieving. Each step we take to build gratitude into our lives will create the space to bring gratitude into our grieving. Every "thank you," every memory, and every tradition allows our loved ones to touch our hearts once again. And in return, as we open those grateful hearts, those connections are transformed. We experience healing as these relationships live on in new ways.

CHAPTER II

Letting Tears Bring
Healing and Renewal

∽

By Mildred Tengbom

A little girl, dying of leukemia, asked a nurse for a crying doll. Puzzled, the nurse asked, "Why do you want a doll that can cry?" "Because I think Mommy and I need to cry," the little girl said. "Mommy won't cry in front of me, and I can't cry if Mommy doesn't. If we had a crying doll, all three of us could cry together. I think we'd feel better then."

I've found crying can make me feel better, too, when sorrow fills my heart. Through death I have lost two sisters, both parents, two sons, aunts and uncles, and some of my dearest friends. I've "lost" homes because of moves.

I've experienced many other losses too. And each time it has felt so good to cry!

I know tears aren't for women only, either. In *Lament for a Son*, Nicholas Wolterstorff relates

9

that he found himself crying after his son died in a climbing accident.

Wolterstorff wrote: "Our culture says men must be strong and that the strength of a man in sorrow is to be seen in his tearless face. Tears are for women. Tears are signs of weakness and women are permitted to be weak. But must we always mask our suffering? I mean, may we not sometimes allow people to see and enter it? May *men* not do this?"

Working your way through | Tears are not a sign of weakness but a sign of strength. Our tears testify to our love. And loving calls for great courage, for in loving we always risk getting hurt.

We cry—women and men—because we've lost someone or something precious. While every loss is an invitation to new life, growth is always scary. But the tears that spring from our love can help us find healing and renewal.

And with healing comes new courage, enabling us to say, "I am determined to honor myself and those I love by going on and living!"

❧ *Let your tears alert you to problems you need to deal with.* Sometimes we cry because we're angry, afraid, guilty, helpless, worn out, or just generally depressed. It's normal to feel this way when grieving a loss, but if you are crying excessively and time isn't bringing relief, you need to try to find out why by asking yourself some questions:

At whom am I angry and why? Do I need to forgive? Are my guilt feelings normal ones of regret or more serious? Is not eating properly, not getting sufficient rest or exercise, or not socializing accentuating my normal feelings of depression? What hidden unmet needs do I have?

~ *Go ahead and cry—to relieve stress.* A year ago my husband faced surgery for cancer. During the weeks we were awaiting the outcome, I agonized. What if he should die? The possibility caused me to begin to grieve.

Grieving is extremely stressful. In *The Broken Heart: The Medical Consequences of Loneliness,* James J. Lynch says that people can actually die from broken hearts. The good news is that crying can remove chemicals that build up during emotional stress, according to Gregg Levoy in a *Psychology Today* article.

He writes that the amount of manganese stored in the body affects our moods, and the body stores 30 times as

> *The tears...streamed down, and I let them flow as freely as they would, making of them a pillow for my heart. On them it rested.*
>
> —Augustine, *Confessions IX, 12*

much of manganese in tears as in blood serum. Biochemist William Frey says the lacrimal gland, which determines the flow of tears, concentrates and removes manganese from the body. Frey has also identified three chemicals stored up by stress and released by crying.

Another study at the University of Pittsburgh School of Nursing has shown that healthy people cry more frequently and feel freer to cry than people who suffer from ulcers and colitis. Since both conditions are closely linked with stress, Frey suggests that tears might be a partial solution to relief of these problems. So to cry can be healthy!

"Those that sow in tears shall reap rejoicing."
—Psalm 126:5

❧ *Respect the differences between the ways men and women grieve.* While men who suffer loss feel it just as profoundly as women, men will often express their feelings differently from women. Studies show that men usually are not as verbal as women about their feelings, and women cry about four times as frequently as men.

If tears are to bring healing, men and women need to learn to respect these differences. "I felt my husband didn't care our child had died," a

12

woman said. "When she accused me of this, I was very angry," her husband said. "I lashed back that I wished she'd quit moping around. I had to go to work every day. How could I cry?"

A wise friend helped the woman understand that she couldn't remake her husband into a woman in his reaction. The man allowed his wife to find relief in tears and, eventually, he discovered he could vent his feelings by whamming a punching bag and chopping wood. Some men, however, can also be helped by being given permission to cry and encouraged to seek a support group where they can share their hurt openly.

❧ *Be comforted by the tears of friends.* A friend wrote of how much she dreaded going to church and hearing the announcement of their son's death. "I inwardly braced myself," she wrote. "But in the hush that enveloped the whole congregation I heard someone crying. I was glad then that I was there, for I could feel the love and concern of others. At the end of the service, the tears of many mingled freely with ours, but the tears provided blessed release and comfort."

❧ *Control your crying when you need to.* A friend noticed that crying as she talked to friends over the phone was upsetting her terminally ill son.

So she began recording a message on her phone answering service. She also asked her husband to answer phone calls when he was at home.

Another mother said she realized that not crying in front of her children might give the mistaken message that she hadn't loved their father. But she also understood that crying excessively might frighten them. "So I told them they would see me crying but they shouldn't worry," she said. "I explained that I needed to cry and after a while I would feel happy again."

People employed outside the home soon discover a need to control crying for tears are not received kindly at places of work. "But sometimes with just a little reminder I burst into tears," one woman said.

R. Scott Sullender, author of *Grief and Growth*, believes we save our tears in inner storehouses. When the storehouse gets filled, the tears may overflow at something that appears quite inconsequential. Setting aside time—perhaps on a weekend—for purposeful grieving with understanding friends can help. Handle clothes, smell familiar perfume, play songs formerly sung in the shower, look at pictures, visit the cemetery. This may also help if you would like to cry but haven't been able to.

[Another's] tears are salve on our wounds.
—Nicholas Wolterstorff,
Lament for a Son

"The worst days are anniversaries and holidays," a bereaved mother said. "Days meant to be celebrations of joy now are days of tears." Some adaptations might help to ease over these difficult days: Plan a small service of remembrance. Place flowers in a church, hospital, or rest home. Invite friends or overseas students for dinner. Change some rituals, like opening Christmas gifts at a different time or lighting a candle instead of hanging a stocking.

❧ *Let your tears wash clean the glasses through which you look at life.* Looking at the world through tears during those weeks surrounding my husband's cancer surgery changed me. It helped me to cherish my dear ones more every day, to long to know God better, and to watch for God in the commonplace events of life. I understand better now what is really of consequence. My life has become richer and more focused.

Tears have a way of putting life in perspective. They can actually help you to laugh again. "How can I be crying in the morning and laughing with my friends in the afternoon?" a young woman asked. This bridge-building from sorrow to joy is one of the gifts tears offer. They help you put your loss in a special place. You don't forget your love or your loss, but you are freed to live.

"I knew I had to tell my children I was going to die," a man said. "So one night Mary and I invited them over. I broke the news. We all cried. 'Now we're going to have a barbeque,' I said. The ribs had never tasted as good, the stars had never shone as brightly, and our laughter had never been as genuine, loving, and healing as it was that night."

Take Heart

"He who conceals grief finds no release for it," an old Turkish proverb counsels. But as you open yourself to grief and allow yourself to cry, healing will come.

Our God wants us to be healed—a God who has been called the God of all comfort. The Greek word the apostle Paul used that is translated "comfort" actually means "to come alongside to help." The English word for "comfort" comes from two Latin words meaning "with strength." God does both. He comes alongside us and gives us strength. He understands our sorrow. He weeps with us. And he assures us that joy will come. Trust him.

Chapter III

Why We Need to Tell the Story of the One We Lost

∽

By M. Donna MacLeod

"I don't want to forget my John," Regina said, staring at the photograph of her husband that she brought to our group. "But it's difficult to remember the warmth of his smile, the way he laughed. It's as if he's fading from my memory, piece by piece."

As Regina shared the sorrow that gnawed at her broken heart, it was clear that her love of John did not end with his death. But what do you do with never-ending love after your loved one is gone?

Dr. Elizabeth Kubler-Ross, a pioneer in the study of grief and grieving, found that telling the story of your departed loved one can honor that love, lighten the burden of loss, and bring you healing and consolation. I agree. Some special people listened to my stories after my youngest daughter, Erynne, lost her battle with cancer. Through the grace of God and their caring presence, consolation calmed my broken heart. That same peace of heart is possible for Regina and for you too!

Working your way through

Our ancestors' custom of wearing black during mourning had benefits. It let people know you recently lost someone important in your life. The compassionate ones could then acknowledge your loss, reinforcing that your loss mattered. The exchange often encouraged the telling of your story, allowing others to share in your sorrow.

Today the pain of grieving is just as great. Yet a black armband isn't worn to let others know you are hurting. Without the visible cue, someone who could acknowledge your loss might decide to spare you the distress of speaking of it.

Silence gives the message, whether intended or not, that others aren't interested or it's time to put stories aside and move on. No wonder many feel alone in their grief!

Suffering in silence only intensifies the pain of grieving. You need an outlet for your emotions, a way to think things through, a chance to acknowledge that your spirit may be suffering too. You *can* get through grief. The key is to tell the story. Let's look at some ways to do it.

❧ *Find a good listener.* Not just any listener will do when you are stricken with grief. You need someone willing to be present to your pain and suffering, to enter into it with you as a caring presence. A good listener uses a nod of the head, gentle eye contact, a kind touch that doesn't linger, a relaxed posture that encourages you to take your time as you say what you need to say. Tears don't disturb such a listener who already knows that crying releases some of the painful emotions of grief.

When a good listener speaks, it's to acknowledge your pain, affirm your attempts at coping, or appreciate you as a person. A good listener is willing to hear the same story

Give sorrow words: the grief that does not speak Whispers the o'er-fraught heart and bids it break.
—William Shakespeare, *Macbeth*, Act IV, Scene 3

again and again until you piece together the fragments and make some sense out of them. Sometimes it is in the speaking of words that you finally understand the story hidden deep in your heart. And don't be afraid to share your story with God, the Great Listener, who alone can mend your wounded heart and spirit.

> *"Memory is the treasury and guardian of all things."*
> —Marcus Tullius Cicero,
> *De Oratore*

∾ *Write the story down.* "I never would have written a word about Tommy, my son who died in Afghanistan," Teresa told the group, "but my daughter, Janine, married a terrific guy who wants to know all the details about her growing up with Tommy. Writing helps me focus on the good times." By putting pen to paper, Teresa discovered another way to connect to fond memories. By recording her motherly perspective, the story of her children linked a new family member to the past and helped others share their own stories.

Perhaps you would rather write a letter to your deceased loved one to say things that you didn't get to say. Or you could send a consoling note to someone who is grieving the loss you are. Or you could keep a daily journal of your grief journey. Just let the spirit within you speak from your heart.

On holidays and anniversaries of Erynne's birth and death, I find myself writing to her—sometimes a note, a letter, a poem, or a snippet about her all-too-brief life. The collection is woven with love. The sadness that could have blotted out the joy of knowing her became an opportunity of grace and growth that continues through the years. So don't be afraid to pick up a pen or pound away at a keyboard. It helps you heal.

❧ *Be creative.* "I love this," Angela said, holding up a throw pillow so everyone in the circle could see its quilted cover. "I made it from Ted's favorite flannel shirts that I just couldn't give away." You could tell by the way she ran her fingers over the neatly stitched patches of plaid, she found great comfort in touching it. And in moments of deep sorrow, she had something of his to hug, to hold close to her aching heart.

Perhaps you have a talent that could capture the essence of your loved one. You may have made a picture

For love is strong as death . . .
—Song of Songs 8:6b

board for the wake or funeral service. Now might be the time to transform it into a scrapbook that has touchable articles that add texture to the memories.

Beyond everyday items, consider how you can honor something that your loved one treasured. It might be a wedding band, a favorite pipe, a locket, a baseball cap, a Bible, a prayer card, or something collectible. Jack told us about his father's rosary, saying, "I keep it on my nightstand as a reminder to pray before sleep like he used to do. I think he'd smile if he knew I take after him."

You might get inspired by something your loved one was known for. Bertha shared that her mother was a great cook: "After she died, I discovered her secret recipes on old index cards. I typed them for my sisters as a Christmas present. Now when the whole family gathers for a holiday, we celebrate with Mum's dishes and tell our favorite stories about her."

Sometimes grief can sap all your energy, leaving you without a creative thought. Be gentle with yourself. Maybe you can't sew a special pillow or hunt for secret recipes, but you might be able to light a candle for your loved one or find peace by sitting in his or her favorite armchair. Any act to acknowledge the one you lost may lift your spirit.

❧ *Honor your loved one.* You can celebrate the life of your departed loved one with others. Alice told us, "It's been years since little Johnny died, but our family still gathers around a cake with candles on his birthday." On special occasions you could offer a toast, place flowers on a grave or scattering site, worship God to give thanks for your life together, or attend a remembrance service at a hospice, bereavement group, or place of worship. Or you could have your loved one's name put on a lasting memorial such as a remembrance wall, wooden walkway to a favorite beach, or bench at a shrine.

You can also honor your loved one through annual community outreach. My family has. In Erynne's memory, her Uncle Colin organizes a neighborhood fund drive for cancer research. Every fall, my oldest, Meganne, gathers her family to walk for the children's hospital where Erynne was treated. This brings in donations for suffering children, and lets our new family members share in Meganne's love of her sister. About a year after Erynne died, my husband Bryan helped me organize a church bereavement ministry that evolved into a lifelong commitment to the brokenhearted. You never know where telling your story will lead you.

Take Heart | Telling the story of the one you lost is a fitting way to honor the life and love you shared with each other. As you wait in faith for the Kingdom to come, take heart in the words of St. John Chrysostom: "Those whom we love and lose are no longer where they were before. They are now wherever we are."

CHAPTER IV

Cherishing Your Memories of a Loved One

∾

By Linus Mundy

There is so much I can't and don't want to forget about the losses in my life. My father comes to mind first. A man of 70 years, he died on Father's Day in 1985. I was once rereading one of my favorite books, Ernest Hemingway's *The Old Man and the Sea,* and I came upon the simple line: "The old man had taught the boy to fish and the boy loved him."

Strong and cherished feelings and memories about my father arose inside of me. My dad may never have taught me much about the fine arts and sciences, but he did teach this boy to fish. And I loved him.

Only a month before Dad died, I asked him to help me carve some "figure-four triggers" for a simple rabbit trap like the ones he and I used to set when I was a youngster. I wanted to share this quaint little contraption with my own children, even if we were only to enjoy the thrill of seeing life up close and then setting the trapped animal free. I also wanted to give my children an experience of what it was like in my father's time, when families hunted and trapped for food.

As he and I got started on the project, Dad winced with the pain of his illness as he carved the trigger sticks. Yet the whole time he knew just what we were up to together: we were making and preserving precious memories; somehow trying to immortalize what he and I had enjoyed together years earlier, what he and his father had enjoyed years before that.

Working your way through | Memories are personal. Whether it's simply speaking the name of your beloved one, holding a ceremony to honor his or her memory, or revisiting a favorite place or activity you shared, the key is to make and preserve connections. Here are a few ideas—my own as well as borrowed ones—to help you strengthen cherished connections with someone you have loved and continue to love.

❧ *Don't hide the hardship.* Loss is painful—that's no secret. Memories, too, can be painful, "but you need to tell your story," says Charlotte Hrubes, co-founder of Joyful Again!, a recovery program for widows and widowers. She urges people not to hide the hardships of their losses, but to share them in a group. "You need to be real somewhere, because other people in your life will probably avoid talking about it. At support groups you can share your feelings....It helps to hear others express the same feelings you've been wrestling with. People who sign up for our sessions invariably tell us, 'No one can have ever felt this much pain.' But then they hear others say the same thing in the group....They gain the strength of realizing they are normal."

Being "normal" means wanting validation for a full range of feelings that loss brings. For example, it is normal for even your closest friends and relatives (and,

> *You will not be cured, but...one day—an idea that will horrify you now—this intolerable misfortune will become a blessed memory of a being who will never again leave you.*
>
> —Marcel Proust, *Letters*

yes, you yourself, too) not to speak the name of the one you've loved and lost. Somehow we have it within our power to pretend that someone we loved deeply and intimately must never have even existed.

"The highest tribute to the dead is not grief but gratitude."

—Thornton Wilder

When my sister begins to talk about our mother, who has died, I answer back that my little Patrick sure is growing up quickly. If my wife happens to mention the miscarriage we experienced just two months before my father's death, I'm quick to end the conversation and hide the hardship.

Some parts of grief have to be let out. Our grief needs to be observed by others. Says Donna O'Toole, a noted grief author, publisher, and teacher: "Grieving our losses does not disconnect us from life but rather, like invisible threads, the losses of our lives weave life unto life."

∽ *Don't hide the hope and the joy.* It is also no secret that love is stronger than death. That is something to celebrate. Ask any of those who have loved and lost and have begun to heal. They remember the death, but they remember the love more. And their fondest wish is that their loved ones now be at peace, in a place of joy. For me, at this time in my life, I have a clear hope in such an outcome after death. But I'm also ready to acknowledge that for many people there is much mystery and doubt about it all.

Arie Brouwer was a theologian who served as General Secretary of the National Council of Churches. He died in 1993. Seeing his death coming, he spoke of faith and hope as mysterious yet very real. He said, "This experience of hope in spite of everything is to me even more important than the experience of faith in spite of everything. However mysterious, I am profusely grateful for both."

We, too, must learn to remain grateful for the love and joy we not only shared with our loved ones but may still be blessed with through our memories of them and our hopes for them. If your belief system gives you the added comfort, joy, and trust that all is well with your loved one now in paradise, indeed

All that we know about those we have loved and lost is that they would wish us to remember them with more intensified realization of their reality. What is essential does not die but clarifies.

—Thornton Wilder

that is a further blessing to celebrate. If you struggle with doubts and fears, talking with a trusted friend, counselor, or minister may be of comfort and help.

❧ *Keep your loved one's finest qualities alive.* This can be your ongoing gift to the one you love, and his or her ongoing gift to the world.

At the burial rite for my father, friends and family were solemnly filing by the casket, giving a final blessing. Some stopped to offer a handshake, a hug, or a word of comfort to our grieving family. "There will never be another one like him," I offered to one of my dearest friends. Her response was a simple: "*You're* just like him." I've never forgotten those beautiful, spontaneous words. And I try to live by them, difficult as it is for me.

"Imitation is the highest form of flattery," goes the saying. The greatest lessons our loved ones have taught us can be beautifully and repeatedly shared. We pay great honor to our loved one's finest qualities by trying to live and act on them in and through our own lives.

You knew your loved one well. Ask yourself: what were the special traits and virtues you learned from her or him that you can help per-petuate by actively developing and sharing them? The world needs all it can get of the good and unique things your loved one possessed and shared. These traits now belong to you—and to the ages—if you act to keep them alive. What a tribute and testament! What a gift to the world!

❧ *Use simple ceremony and ritual.* Ceremony and ritual are especially helpful for remembering our loved ones. "Whenever we experience a transition, happy or sad, a ceremony helps us recenter ourselves by making a symbolic statement about that change," writes Lynda Paladin in *Ceremonies for Change.*

Betty Hopf, a Sister of Providence and a chaplain with a special gift for grief ministry, gives workshops on remembering. "It is more painful to try to forget than to remember," she says. Here are just a sampling of her ideas and suggestions.

Bring a favorite picture of your deceased loved one to a family gathering and explain why it's special to you, what memories it brings to mind for you. Others often will chime in with their memories.

Visit the cemetery as a group and bring a flower that symbolizes some special trait about your loved one. "Mary taught me to stop and smell the roses"; "John brought new life and sunshine to so many."

Invent your own simple rituals, individually or together with family and close friends.

Take Heart | In *The Angel Who Forgot,* Elisa Barton tells the story of an angel who can heal ailing children. The angel loses his beloved pony in the forest and is so sad he can't bear to remember it. To stop the hurt, the angel throws all his memories away. But now he can't remember how to help others and cannot heal a young child who needs him. With the help of a wise parent, the angel's memories are recovered and the angel once again is whole, once again able to heal others.

Heal and be healed. Remember.

CHAPTER V

The Other Side of Grief

෨

By Darcie Sims

Will we ever be happy again? How long does grief last and will I ever get over it, and if I do, what then? You have been grieving for some time now and may have grown weary of the tears, sadness, and emptiness that often accompany grief. Perhaps you are wondering if it will ever end.

You have probably discovered that grief is an injury—a severe and devastating emotional, psychological, physical, and spiritual wound that causes great pain and trauma. Yet, eventually, over a period of time, that injury does heal and you must then learn to live with the scar that is left. Grief is a process and nothing stays the same. Even if you feel you have remained stuck in the same hurting place, you *have moved* forward. You are continually making progress even when you temporarily slide backward or sideways.

You will continue to grieve your losses throughout your life, but it doesn't have to have the same intensity or duration as earlier grief. Just as you have changed, so too has your grief; and, it is now time to explore the possibilities that lie on the *other side of grief.*

Working your way through | In our early grief, we may get caught in viewing the world in terms of what we no longer have. We keep mental lists of the things we will never know or experience. Sometimes, when all we think we have left of our love is our sadness, we don't want to give up our grief for fear of giving up our loved one. But, letting go of grief doesn't mean that you no longer miss loved ones. They are a part of your life forever, but their role in your life has changed.

We can, however, choose how we wish grief to influence us. We can carry bitterness and anger, or we can choose to remember the light and the love. And each day we draw a breath, we have that choice again and again.

❧ *A change in our surroundings.* We rearrange the furniture, change rooms, sometimes we move. *"THE ROOM"* becomes a den, a sewing room, a guest room, or perhaps someone else's room. We slowly begin to understand that putting our loved one's things away does not mean putting him or her out of our life!

❧ *Special remembrances.* Some families attach significance to special symbols. They adopt a favorite song, animal, color, or object that helps remind them of their loved one. These symbols are used to help trigger good memories and act as connections to their loved one. For some, they help ease the painful memories into gentle reminders of the love that was shared. Symbols remind us of the love we cherish and give us something to hold on to when the grief grows strong and the night too long.

❧ *Be prepared for recurring grief.* Sometimes you may feel as though you have slipped backwards and that nothing

You are the part of love that never goes away.
—Alicia S. Franklin,
Am I Still a Sister

will ever get better. You may retreat back into acute grief. As you retrace your steps through the valley of grief, however, you may notice that your despair feels different. Perhaps it seems to last a shorter length of time...the gloom seems to fade more quickly. There may be laughter this time in spite of your renewed grief.

∾ *Making the choice to LIVE again.* You will wrestle long and hard and finally discover the awful truth of grief: your loved one, your child, your spouse, your parent, your sibling, your friend has DIED. You have NOT. You are left among the living, to carve out an existence that must experience not only the pains of life, but the joys as well. And suddenly, survival isn't enough. If you are to be in this life, then you can choose to LIVE again.

*"A time will come when you will want to laugh and live and love again.
Let yourself heal—in your own time and your own way."*

—Robert DiGiulio,
Losing Someone Close

This now becomes a fork in the road...a *choice point* between grieving forever or learning to live with what you've got instead of what you wanted. You don't have to remember only the awfulness of the death. You can choose to recall the joys, the light your loved one brought, the music of his presence in your life. You do not have to depend upon symbols to remind you of the life and the joy and love you shared. Remember that your loved one lives within your heart and not in the symbol you have chosen to cherish. You may eventually "retire" that special symbol and not have to have it close at hand as you reach for the other side of grief.

You will find new ways to remember the life, to rekindle the magic that was shared between you. Learn to release the darkness in hope of there being light...in spite of the terribleness of the storms you have endured.

❧ *Progress on your journey.* Some say the path to healing begins when we learn to say good-bye. Good-bye to what? To whom? Good-bye to our loved one? We can say good-bye to the life we lived together, but never, ever to the memories

> Grief isn't a seasonal song. It's a lifetime song. But it doesn't have to be a sad song forever.
>
> —Darcie D. Sims,
> *Touchstones*

and the moments of the life we shared! We can pick and choose how those memories affect us and just knowing we have choices is the beginning of the "other side of grief."

So how do you know when you are approaching the other side of grief? What is progress and what does it look like? You know you're making progress through grief when:

- You don't always choke up when you say your loved one's name.
- Tears don't always well up in your eyes when you think of your loved one.
- The CAUSE of death isn't the emphasis anymore.
- You begin to tell less of the death story and more of the LIFE story of your loved one.
- Memories, for the most part, bring comfort, not pain.
- You realize your plans don't include your loved one any more.
- You realize you can never go back to the "old" you…you have a "new normal."
- You can forgive yourself for living.
- The death of your loved one is no longer CAPITALIZED and written in neon.
- Hope begins to return when you can hear laughter again…and some of that laughter is your own.

- You no longer become angry with others for being happy.
- You KNOW that even though your loved one died, the love between you can never be destroyed.
- The "other side of grief" begins when you wake up one morning and remember FIRST that your loved one lived, not just that he died.

Take Heart The "other side of grief" is not freedom from pain, nor is it a return to the original picture.

It is acknowledging and living your grief. It is finally understanding that we don't get over grief...we get *through* it.

Healing is possible when we discover a smile flickering across our face, when memories bring warmth and comfort rather than tears and pain. Healing begins to occur when we can learn to *reinvest* our energies, emotions, and love rather than seek to *replace* it. When we completely understand that we did not *lose* our loved ones, healing is possible.

Life can become good and whole and complete once again...not when we try to fill up the empty spaces left by loved ones no longer within hug's reach, but when we realize that love creates new spaces in the heart and expands the spirit and deepens the joy of simply being alive.

And that renewed energy and love become the memorials to our loved ones—not the grave markers we decorate, not the books we write, not the speeches we give, but the LOVE we share and pass on.

About the Authors

Lisa Irish, MEd, MA, BCC, *is a chaplain, spiritual director, and writer in Connecticut. She is currently learning from and ministering to bereaved folks at Yale New Haven Hospital.*

Mildred Tengbom *has written more than 20 books, including* Grief for a Season. *She and her husband, Dr. Luverne Tengbom, have served as missionaries in East Africa, Nepal, and recently Singapore. They have four grown children.*

M. Donna MacLeod, RN, MSN, *is the author of* Seasons of Hope Guidebook: Creating and Sustaining Catholic Bereavement Groups *and companion* Participant Journals. *She has also written* CareNotes *and* PrayerNotes *on grief.*

Linus Mundy *founded* One Caring Place *in 1988, and has written numerous titles in the* CareNotes *series. In 2013, he received a Lifetime Achievement Award from the Association of Catholic Publishers. His two newest books are entitled* Simply Merton *and* Comfort My People: Prayers for Chaplains.

Darcie D. Sims, Ph.D., C.H.T., C.T., G.M.S., *is a bereaved parent, a grief management specialist, a nationally certified thanatologist, a certified pastoral bereavement specialist, a board certified professional counselor, and a licensed psychotherapist and hypnotherapist. She is director of the* American Grief Academy® *in Seattle, Washington, and the author of numerous books and grief resources. She can be contacted at* www.griefinc.com.

CaringCompanions
from Abbey Press

**These books gather themes published
in our *CareNotes* series and present
them in five chapters.**

Available at your favorite gift shop or bookstore—
or directly from Abbey Press Publications,
St. Meinrad, IN 47577.
Call 1-800-325-2511.
www.abbeypresspublications.com